CW01481513

Being Active:
A Guide for Hypnotherapy
Weight Control Clients

Prof. Stuart Biddle

and

Fiona Biddle

UK Academy of Therapeutic Arts and Sciences Ltd.

©UK Academy of Therapeutic Arts and Sciences, Stuart Biddle & Fiona Biddle 2010

Published by

UK Academy of Therapeutic Arts and Sciences Ltd
16 St Philips Rd, Burton on the Wolds, Loughborough, LE12 5TS
Tel: 01509 881811
Email: info@ukacademy.org
Internet: www.ukacademy.org

ISBN 0-9544604-0-5

Note
Neither the publishers nor the authors will be liable for any loss or damage of any nature occasioned to or suffered by any person acting or refraining from acting as a result of reliance on the material contained in this publication.

Printed in the UK by Lightning Source

2

For Jack and Greg,
with love

Contents

About the authors

Stuart Biddle, PhD, CPsychol

After a first degree in Physical Education and Social Studies at Loughborough University, Professor Biddle studied the Psychology of Sport & Physical Activity at the Pennsylvania State University. He has been lecturing in higher education since 1979, during which time he gained a PhD in Psychology. He is currently Professor of Exercise and Sport Psychology at Loughborough University. He was Head of their School of Sport and Exercise Sciences , 2001-07.

His main interests are in behavioural aspects of physical inactivity, activity and health, including motivational and emotional aspects of physical activity and exercise and recent publications have been on children's physical activity, sedentary behaviour, and motivation.

In 1999 he completed an 8-year term as President of the European Federation for the Psychology of Sport and Physical Activity and was President of the International Society of Behavioural Nutrition and Physical Activity 2009-10. He has been Chair of the Scientific Committee of the European College of Sport Science. In 1998, Professor Biddle received the Distinguished International Scholar Award from the

7

Association for the Advancement of Applied Sport Psychology in the USA for his work in exercise and health psychology, and in 2003 was the Pease family scholar at Iowa State University. Current and recent research projects have been sponsored by the British Heart Foundation, NHS Health Scotland, Masterfoods, Esporta Health Clubs, and the Medical Research Council.

Stuart's main forms of physical activity are active travel and golf: Fiona sometimes thinks he lives at the golf club (with both sons!)

 **Fiona Biddle,** BSc, DipCouns, HPD, ADHP(NC), ECP, FNCH, UKCP(H)

Fiona has been a hypnotherapist since 1993. She is also a psychotherapist, counsellor and professional coach. She co-developed a new model of therapy: the Motivational Model of Hypnotism. In addition to her private practice, which has offices in Loughborough and London, she is Vice-Principal of the UK Academy of Therapeutic Arts and Sciences, Managing Director of the National College of Hypnosis and Psychotherapy, Chair of the UKCP College of Hypno-psychotherapy, an ex-Chair of both the National Council for Hypnotherapy and the UK Confederation of Hypnotherapy Organisations and in 2002 was one of the 8 practitioners chosen to serve on the Technical Working Group to write the government approved National Occupational Standards for Hypnotherapy. Fiona also co-designed

8

the Nationally Accredited Hypnotherapy Practitioner Diploma as well as the Certificate in Hypnotherapeutic Supervision. She has co-authored the books "Building a Successful and Ethical Therapy Practice", "Motivational Hypnotism" and "Hypnotic Coaching".

Fiona's main form of physical activity is cycling: a time when she can think, and escape from the phone and emails.

How to use this book

This book is written to help you understand moving from thinking about being physically active to maintaining an active lifestyle. It may be that you are already active, but could do with being more so, or you may really dislike the idea of building activity into your life. There could be many other alternatives, and this book is designed to work with you and help you meet your goals.

This is an active book in every way and you will have plenty of opportunities to complete check lists and questionnaires, answer questions, and to think about your own lifestyle. All of these things have been included to help make the book lively, interesting and, above all, successful in helping you achieve the levels of physical activity in your life that you feel comfortable with!

The book starts with an introduction about physical activity, and then goes into the benefits of a physically active lifestyle. Practical tips are then outlined for how to get started, keeping going, avoiding quitting, and getting started again after a break.

We look at how attitudes and beliefs affect a person's tendency to be active, how to set goals, how to enjoy the process (yes, you can!) and how to build your confidence.

In addition, we go on to say a few things about different types of people and how this might affect the advice we give. These groups include children, adults, older adults, men and women.
Finally, other parts of a healthy lifestyle are also covered in this book. These include your diet, smoking habits and control of stress.

Introduction

We all have good intentions - the 'New Year Resolution' syndrome! What happens? We start off in a blaze of glory and good intentions, and then.... we tail off in our efforts and soon revert back to where we were!

Why should this be?

We must all realize that the behaviours we adopt as humans are based on whether we <u>have</u> to do them or whether we <u>choose</u> to do them. It is the choice behaviours that we have so much trouble with, especially if we find them difficult to fit in, or they are less than enjoyable at times.

Let's take an example. Few people have trouble choosing their favourite meal and eating it. This is because it is immediately reinforcing and enjoyable. But, to say to someone that they must avoid their favourite foods is a different matter altogether. Now they have real trouble and require strong motivation, help from friends, good planning etc.

The point is that it is not easy to choose a behaviour that initially appears to be 'unpleasant' or unrewarding, like depriving yourself of your favourite foods. Another point here is why are your trying to avoid these foods? It is probably because you are hoping to lose weight. We all know that this takes time. So, you are trying to avoid the nice foods you eat every day so that you look better in several months time. Wow, you must be strong-willed to go through all of that, mustn't you? This is something that your hypnotherapist will be helping you to deal with. They can help you to keep that motivation going, and to make eating healthily as pleasant and fulfilling as possible.

The same sort of feelings can occur when thinking of physical activity. Many people (you?) think that physical activity and exercise is unpleasant and that benefits will take several weeks and months to show, so it just ain't worth it! Right?

Wrong!

Absolutely wrong!

And this is where we come in. With many years of practical, academic and professional experience between us in both the promotion of physical activity for health, and hypnotherapy, we are able to help you plan for a physically active life using techniques that are well used and respected in health promotion, health and physical education, psychology and medicine. Your hypnotherapist can help you to instil new behaviours and to make these processes, just as with eating, as pleasant and fulfilling as possible.

Stuart's book 'Psychology of physical activity' gives the academic stuff - here we give you the down-to-earth practical tips and information you need to start and maintain physical activity .... for now and for life!

KNOWLEDGE QUIZ

Now we would like to ask you a few questions to find out how much you know about health and physical activity. All you have to do is answer true or false to these questions:

1.   The following are all aerobic activities if carried out for around twenty minutes: brisk walking, jogging, cycling, swimming.

2.   3-5 periods of brisk walking, of about 30 mins, each week will reduce the risk of coronary heart disease.

3.   Osteoporosis is a muscle that can be strengthened through exercise.

4.   Once you reach your 60th birthday it is no longer safe to exercise.

---

5.   Over 150,000 people die each year in England and Wales of heart disease.

6.   Having a sauna is a good way to lose weight because of how much you sweat.

7.   Pregnant women should avoid all exercise.

8.   Scientific studies show that physical activity can help people who suffer from depression and anxiety.

9.   For a physical activity session to help your heart, you must push yourself until it hurts and 'go for the burn'.

10.   As long as you are physically active it is healthy to keep eating fatty foods.

Answers:
1. True
2. True
3. False. Osteoporosis is a medical condition of the thinning of the bones associated with mineral loss, usually most acute after the menopause. See p35

4. False. People of all ages can and should exercise. You may not be able to exercise at the same pace, and extra medical advice would be sensible but the benefits are still there for you.

5. True.

6. False. Sweating simply loses water and salt from the body which will be relaced very quickly. Permanent weight loss should be from loss of body fat which can only be obtained through a combination of dietary control and physical activity.

7. False. It is generally recommended that pregnant women can continue with exercise that they are used to for as long as is comfortable. Medical advice should be sought.

8. True.

9. False. Research has shown that moderate forms of exercise can give significant benefits to health.

10. False. Fatty foods should only be eaten in moderation, however healthy the other aspects of your life.

Physical activity has always been recognized as important, whether it be for health, sport, work or survival. Some like it, some don't, but one thing is true - we need it! Humans were born to move and, until the second half of the 20th century, we moved quite a lot. This was mainly in our jobs and doing everyday tasks that machines now do for us.

Have a think for a moment of how mechanised our lives are now. We have TV remote controls, power steering and automatic windows in our cars; we often drive when we could easily walk. There are lifts and escalators all over the place, and sometimes we are even told NOT to walk. In our local shopping centre there is a moving walkway, which specifically says "do not walk"! How ridiculous is that?

Does this matter? Evidence shows that it certainly does matter and that the diseases of earlier times, like typhoid and smallpox - infectious diseases - have given way to diseases of inactivity. These include coronary heart disease, obesity and diabetes.

Clarification of Terms

Before we explain a little more about this, let's first look at the different terms that we will use throughout this book. What do they mean?

Physical Activity

This is all movement of the body produced by the muscles. This could be very vigorous movement with a high expenditure of energy, like sports training, or mild activity with very little energy expended, like sitting at a desk typing. For our purposes, physical activity refers to all body movement requiring exertion <u>above</u> resting levels.

Exercise

This is physical activity that is usually done in a structured and often repetitive way with the aim of getting or keeping fit. For example, exercise might include jogging, dancing, keep-fit classes, cycling, some sports etc.

Sport

Sport is those exercises that are performed in a competitive, structured and rule-governed way. They involve physical movement (often quite large amounts of movement), strategy, prowess and chance. We do not, therefore, include recreational activities such as cycling or jogging as 'sport', at least not until they become part of a competition.

Physical fitness

We all know what physical fitness means don't we? Try to tell someone, without reading on, what physical fitness is.

It's not easy is it?

An American professor once said that physical fitness was something that people 'have or achieve' in helping them to perform physical activity. This is an important definition because of two words: 'have' and 'achieve'. This tells us that physical fitness can be obtained through two routes:

a.   the 'have' route: some people possess quite high 'natural' fitness or potential for high performance in physical activities; these are the natural athletes we came across at school. If they carried on training and practicing, they were probably successful in sport.

b.   the 'achieve' route: all of us will gain in physical fitness through participation in physical activity, although this will depend on the amount and type of activities, of course. You do not need to be a natural athlete to do this. All of us need to achieve some level of fitness to enhance our health.

Physical fitness can also be broken down into different parts. Some parts of fitness are more related to good health than others, while some are more related to performance in activities like sport.

Health-Related Fitness

Parts of fitness called 'health-related' are:

- aerobic (stamina) fitness
- muscle strength
- muscle endurance
- muscle flexibility
- amount of body fat
- stress control

Why are these health-related?

Because low levels of each of these parts of fitness have been associated with some health problems. For example, those low in aerobic (stamina) fitness may be at greater risk of coronary heart disease, and this is also true for those high in body fat. Poor muscle tone (strength and endurance) may create problems with posture and bring about back ache or muscle injuries.

Physical activity or exercise that help these parts of fitness is called 'health-related exercise' and might include walking (for fat control), jogging or dancing (for stamina), and muscle toning (for strength).

Skill-Related Fitness

There are also parts of fitness that are more related to performing well and skilfully. These are:

- agility
- balance
- coordination
- power
- reaction time
- speed

These are sometimes called components of 'motor fitness' and they help us perform physical activities more proficiently. However, they do not directly affect health in the sense of preventing or reducing the risk of disease. In other words, those with poor skill-related fitness are not at any risk of health problems because of this, whereas those poor in aspects health-related exercise/fitness can be at greater risk of certain health problems.

Health

People often talk about the health benefits of physical activity. One of the problems though is actually defining health in the first place. Health is a continuum from low to high mental, physical and social well-being, and not just the absence of disease. Positive health might be termed positive well-being or high level 'wellness' (a bit of an

Americanism but quite a good word if you think about it).

Most people though only talk about physical activity in the way that it might help prevent or offset diseases or 'problems'.

Hypnosis

Hypnosis is a natural and normal state of focussed attention. When in hypnosis, you are still aware and able to do anything you would normally be able to do, and your hypnotist cannot make you do anything you wouldn't!

However, it is a powerful state in which the deeper levels of mind can decide to make changes to habits, behaviours or beliefs and so it is a valuable state to use to help with such issues as weight control and becoming physically active.

Hypnosis can be utilised to help you find your motivation to do things differently and to build your belief in yourself and your confidence in your abilities.

Hypnotherapy

Hypnotherapy is the clinical application of hypnosis to assist clients to resolve problems arising from habits, maladaptive behaviours, pain (under medical supervision) and psychosomatic medical conditions. It can also be used to assist clients in maximising potential in settings such as work and sport.

Hypnotherapists should be trained to a level 4 NVQ equivalent standard. Hypnotherapists are not trained to deal with deep psychological issues or psychiatric illness.

Psychotherapy

Psychotherapy is defined by the United Kingdom Council of Psychotherapy as a process "to help clients gain insight into their difficulties or distress, establish a greater understanding of their motivation, and enable them to find more appropriate ways of coping or bring about changes in their thinking and behaviour. Psychotherapy involves exploring feelings, beliefs, thoughts and relevant events, sometimes from childhood and personal history, in a structured way."

Hypno-psychotherapy

Hypno-psychotherapy is the clinical application of hypnosis to enhance psychotherapeutic interventions. Hypno-psychotherapists should be trained at masters level and are trained to deal with deep psychological issues and psychiatric illness.

Other words and terms

Frequency

How many times you exercise each week. This may be important for scheduling exercise sessions, although we recommend that you be as physically active as possible and not just in 'exercise sessions'.

Intensity

How intense the physical activity is, such as light, moderate or hard.

Duration

How long any one period of physical activity lasts.

The benefits of physical activity

You must have noticed that physical activity has become big business and popular in magazines and newspapers.

Where were the glamorous health and fitness clubs 30 years ago?

Where were the mass fun runs and marathons then?

Why has this big change happened?

One reason is that people in countries like Britain and the USA have become less active over the past few decades. Although there is very little data to compare, say, activity levels at the beginning of the 20th century with those now, it is fairly obvious that the opportunities for physical activity have changed. The most obvious change has been at work where activity has declined with greater automation - the term 'laboursaving devices' sums it up quite nicely!

This has meant that if people who previously had been active at work want to maintain their levels of activity, they must choose to be active in their own leisure time. Also the increase in the availability of motorised transport has had a huge effect. For example, Fiona remembers her grandmother saying that she would walk a mile to take her daughters to school, and a mile home, then pick them up for lunch and take them back, and finally pick them up at the end of the school day. That makes eight miles a day, five days a week! Plus of course, her trips to the shops etc.

An interesting study recently reported on the 'Amish' community in Canada. These people adopt lifestyles similar to what we all had in the 19th century- no electrical devices or cars, and a subsistence farming existence. The study showed very high levels of physical activity and very little overweight or obesity.

Are we physically active?

Trying to measure physical activity is very difficult. However, research suggests that about 20% of the British and American adult population take part in sufficient physical activity to improve their health.

It has also been reported that about 40% of adults take no real physical activity at all, while the other 40% do some activity now and again.

Some people have suggested that even children have low levels of physical activity. Children are more active than many adults, but probably don't take part in vigorous activity for long periods of time. This will be particularly true for younger children. Children today have many appealing sedentary things to do, like play computer games. In some cases this will detract from being physically active. Concern about safety when out alone, or when riding bikes also hasn't helped.

So, with less activity as part of our lives, people have looked towards creating their own activity, like going to keep-fit classes, jogging and then running in local fun runs, going to dance groups, or following home exercise videos. Others have chosen to integrate physical activity into their lives by cycling to work or walking more.

But does physical activity do us any good?

What about the media hype concerning heart attacks and muscle injuries? This part of the book will summarize for you the potential benefits of exercise and physical activity.

The benefits

Mental health

When we refer to mental health, we simply mean feeling good. One of the most widely stated benefits that participants in regular physical activity report is that they 'feel good'. This is related, of course, to enjoyment of the physical activity experience.

Researchers have found that anxiety and depression can be lower for those who are physically active. Also, physical activity can help raise self-esteem (the way we feel about ourselves), particularly if the person feels successful or has had an enjoyable and worthwhile experience.

Large surveys in both Britain and America have shown that people who are physically active have better 'mental health' than those who are less active or who do no activity at all. In fact, the ancient Greeks reported exactly the same, although didn't use questionnaires or opinion polls.

Although the ancient Greeks knew about the mental benefits of physical activity, it was not until more modern research that we were able to identify what was going on. Physical activity seems to be able to effect our 'mental health' as follows:

- reduced anxiety
- reduced depression
- increased self-esteem
- better mood

Why is this?

Well, we are not too sure exactly why these things can occur. However, we do know that after physical activity, muscle tension can be reduced, and this can have a relaxing effect.

Try it!

When you feel really tired at the end of the day, try doing about 15-20 minutes of physical activity. Do you feel more tired? Probably not. Most people report feeling less tired, more alert, but pleasantly relaxed.

Other possible reasons why we might feel better physical activity, and enjoy exercising, include:

- chemical changes in the brain that make us feel better
- improved ability to handle stress when we are physically fitter
- ability to do more things with more energy
- greater independence
- feeling of satisfaction, self-improvement etc.

These effects are possible for all people of all ages But, there will be some types of activity that just don't appeal to you. Fine! Choose something else! If you find the right activity, these effects should occur.

Coronary heart disease

Reduction in the risk of coronary heart disease (CHD) is usually the most commonly mentioned health benefit of physical activity. It is now well known that regular and appropriate physical activity can reduce this risk. This makes exercise/activity a very cheap and effective way of reducing Britain's current leading cause of early death.

How do we know CHD can be related to a lack of physical activity? The 'classic' community studies of

CHD and physical activity involved people in sedentary and active jobs.

For example, Professor Jerry Morris studied people in London delivering post and compared them to the office workers who were quite inactive. Professor Ralph Paffenbarger looked at dockyard workers in San Francisco and compared active with less active workers in terms of CHD.

These studies, and many more as well, found that levels of physical activity were related to signs of CHD and actual heart attacks. This research led Dr Kenneth Powell and his colleagues from the Centres for Disease Control in the USA to state as long ago as 1987 that they now believed that physical inactivity was a cause of CHD.

Professor Morris has said that the type of activity required to help reduce the risk of CHD is stamina-type activity for 15 minutes or more several times a week. These types of physical activity range from brisk walking to more vigorous, but prolonged, exercise such as running, cycling, swimming, and some continuous sports.

Professor Paffenbarger has also found that people with high energy output through the day have a lower risk of CHD. It appears, therefore, a generally active lifestyle is important for reducing the risk of CHD.

For most people, it is probably not so important to achieve high levels of physical fitness, although changing from being very unfit to being moderately fit should have a major positive effect on health and well-being. Moving from moderate to high fitness will probably affect physical health a little less.

High Blood Pressure

Moderate aerobic (stamina) physical activity has been shown to reduce high blood pressure. The use of muscle strengthening exercises for those with high blood pressure is more controversial, although recent studies have shown the benefits of properly supervised light resistance exercise.

Those with high blood pressure, or those who think they might have high blood pressure, might like to ask their doctor, but it is quite likely that they will be prescribed moderately brisk physical activity, like walking.

Obesity

Some readers of this book will be among the 20% of the British population who are classified as 'obese' (high bodyfat), and many of the others will have body fat above recommended levels (that is presumably why your hypnotherapist has given you this book!).

Physical activity of a moderate intensity but long duration should enable people to achieve and maintain higher levels of energy expenditure. This will help bodyweight control.

Have you ever been told that physical activity is not good for fat loss because it doesn't use enough calories?
Well, that's right about the calories (energy). Physical activity actually uses quite a small amount when you compare it with some of the foods we eat. For example, to use up the energy from a 4oz pork pie you would need to play tennis for over an hour!

So why bother?

Because if you maintain physical activity, slowly but surely it will help you control your bodyweight.

Here's another example:

Generally, we are creatures of habit. We tend to eat and drink about the same amounts from one week to the next. So, you decide to walk to work twice a week instead of taking the car. This amounts to a total of one hour of walking each week.

If you eat and drink roughly the same over the next year, an average person could lose up to 5 pounds (2.5 kilos) of fat in the year. If you decide to walk three times a week, this will increase to nearly 7 pounds!

Go to the kitchen now and put a one pound slab of butter of margarine on the worktop!

Seven of those just by walking 15 minutes to and 15 minutes back (from work) three days a week for this year. Now isn't that a good deal?

Diabetes

Physical activity has been recommended for the treatment and control of diabetes for many years. The 'treatment triad' often recommended is diet, insulin and physical activity. The link between diabetes and physical activity goes back some time. About 2,500 years!

A Chinese doctor of the Sui Dynasty recommended physical activity, and medical doctors today have continued with the same advice. The opening to Dr Robert Cantu's book on diabetes and exercise is: 'can diet and exercise prevent diabetes? The answer is an emphatic yes'!

People who take little physical activity and are overweight or obese are at higher risk of becoming diabetic.

Osteoporosis

Osteoporosis is the excessive loss of mineral content of the bone and can result in fractures. It is most common in women after the menopause. Weight bearing activities, like walking, are recommended to maintain bone density, so again physical activity is important.

Low Back Pain

Did you know that about 80% of British adults will report suffering back pain at some time in their lives but only 10% will seek medical attention?

Exercises recommended for a healthy back involve the muscles of the pelvis and hip. Good muscle tone in the stomach, low back, and sides of the trunk is important, as well as having flexible muscles of the hamstrings (back of the thigh) and lower back.

Are there any risks of physical activity?

Yes, there are risks and these fall into two main categories:

a.   sudden cardiac death
b.   muscle/bone injuries.

Sudden cardiac death

The newspapers have been quick to highlight the more sensational, yet tragic, aspects of mass exercise events such as marathons. People have died in marathons and on the squash court.

This is hardly surprising when someone is dying every few minutes of CHD in Britain every day of the year! However, the risk of sudden cardiac death is raised during exercise, but the overall balance between cardiac benefit and risk is positive.

Research has shown that men who exercised vigorously for more than 20 minutes each week had an overall risk of cardiac arrest only 40% of their sedentary counterparts.

In other words the inactive men were more at risk than those participating in physical activity! Obviously some people are more at risk than others, and your doctor will be able to advise you.

Injury

The risk of injury to muscles, bones and joints will, of course, depend on the type of activity, as well as the frequency, intensity and duration of involvement. Research suggests that injuries can occur through health-related physical activity, such as jogging, particularly in overweight or older people.

Good preparation through progressive physical activity and warm-up routines, including adequate stretching exercises, is recommended. Also, low impact activities, like walking, are particularly recommended for older or overweight individuals. Correct shoes for jogging, walking, dancing etc. can also help prevent injury.

Summary

Regular physical activity can have a real positive effect on how we feel mentally, and can help in preventing or reducing the risks and effects of

- coronary heart disease
- overweight and obesity
- high blood pressure
- diabetes
- osteoporosis
- low back pain

Some exercise may increase the risk of muscle and joint injuries but sensible precautions will minimize this.

People who do NOT exercise are at much greater risk of dying early than those who do!

Stages of Readiness for Physical Activity

There are many academic theories relevant to physical activity. One relates to people's readiness to be active (called stages of change) and is a useful way to look at changing physical activity levels. The stages are:

Precontemplation

This is the person who has no intention to take action. This may have been (or may still be) you, when you first visited your hypnotherapist. It may be that it was your intention to lose weight just by controlling your food intake. If this is still you, please keep reading as it is our intention to move you on to the next stage.

Intend to be active? No. Active? No.

Contemplation

This is the person who is intending to take action, but hasn't done anything about it yet. This could well be where you are at right now. It may be that you are just now thinking about being more physically active. Is that so? If so, this book can help you to move on through the stages.

Intend to be active? Yes. Active? No.

Preparation

This is the person who intends to take action soon, is deciding how and has begun to take some behavioural steps in this direction. Perhaps this is you. Maybe you are starting to decide what form of activity would suit you, or how to build more into your current lifestyle. In this case, this book can help you to prepare effectively and to move to the action stage.

Intend to be active? Yes. Active? A little perhaps.

Action

This is the person who is in the process of changing their behaviour. This is, or will be, you when you have started to be more active. Perhaps you are gradually building more activity into your life, or trying out different types of activity.

Intend to be active? Yes. Active? Yes (recently).

Maintenance

This is the person who has made the change and is keeping going with new behaviours. This book can help with this process, to keep your motivation going and where possible, to prevent relapse to old behaviours.

Intend to be active? Yes. Active? Yes (for a while).

Contemplation:
I'm thinking about it!

So now you know that being physically more active can make you feel better, help you control your weight and help prevent some of the diseases of the 21st century.

So far, so good. But you've probably heard much of this before. So let's look now at practical information and guidelines to help you get started.

When people ask Stuart at a party what he does for a job, he tells them that he is a university professor. When they ask what he specializes in, he might say 'the psychology of physical activity and health'. "Oh!" - a real conversation stopper. People think that it's a really weird subject.

But just think about it for a moment.

He is interested in people being physically active so that they lead healthy and productive lives. Much of that is to do with motivation, attitudes, confidence, enjoying physical activity, how you feel about yourself, and what you think others feel about you, etc etc ..... isn't it? Putting it into more formal language - the psychology of exercise!

What follows then, are simple messages and strategies based on sound principles of psychology. Nothing mystical or odd - just a mix of knowledge from research, practical experience and good 'ole common sense!

(Incidentally, when Fiona is asked the same question, answering that she is a hypnotherapist is anything but a conversation stopper, so sometimes she says she checks the calculations on submitted VAT returns: no one ever asks anything! She is then free to ask about the other person!)

Being in the stage of contemplation means that the desired levels of physical activity have not been reached but there is an intention to get there.

Attitudes and beliefs

We probably all think that 'positive attitudes' are needed to make changes in our lives. To a certain extent, of course, that is true.

So what are attitudes and how can they help?

Attitudes are about what we think:

- "Spurs will win the Cup this year!" ....
- "I think walking is better for losing weight than playing badminton".

But attitudes are also about the way we feel -
- "I like Spurs" ....
- "I don't like walking".

So, attitude = belief + feeling
But how does this work in practice? Let's take Jane as an example:

- "I think that walking is good for helping me lose weight" (BELIEF)

- "I would like to lose weight" (ATTITUDE & INTENTION)

- "I like walking" (ATTITUDE)

This situation, obviously, is very positive for Jane who wants to lose weight. She has a positive belief and intention about walking and weight loss and she likes to walk. Everything points to Jane walking!

Of course, it's not always quite so simple. Here is another example, Tim:

- "I think jogging will really help me get back in shape"

- "I find jogging hard work and boring"

So, although Tim believes in the physical benefits jogging, he is not so likely to be able to stick with a jogging programme.

Take a little time now to think about your own beliefs and feelings.

Thinking Task

BELIEFS: What are your beliefs about physical activity?

For example, what do think about regular walking, jogging, swimming, some sports, gardening etc etc?

Write some of your beliefs here and remember just to list what you think will be the <u>outcome</u> of your involvement. Number 1 is an example:

1. I think that walking to work at least three days every week will help me control my weight

2.

3.

4.

5..

FEELINGS:
Now take time to list what you feel about these
outcomes and beliefs.

Do you want to lose weight, get fitter etc (if these
were listed above)?
1. I want to keep myself in good shape and keep my
weight under control

2.

3.

4.

5.

From this, plan activities than you feel will produce
an effect that you want. Eliminate activities that
you feel negative about or ones which seem not have
such beneficial effects.

Of course, one good way to have positive beliefs about physical activity is to inform yourself of the benefits. Many people have misunderstood physical activity - read the introduction to this book again to remind yourself of the benefits.

Summary

Attitudes

1.   attitudes include your beliefs - inform yourself of the benefits of activity

2.   attitudes include your feelings - highlight activities you want to do

Support from friends

Support from others- your friends ,family, colleagues etc- will also be important when getting started. Get your friends and family to help; better still, get them to join you!

Most of us like exercising in small groups or with a particular friend. We can all help to motivate each other, particularly at times when one of us doesn't really feel like it! There are some, of course, who find the solitude of exercising alone quite relaxing, or like Fiona, find it gives them time to think!

Social Support Task

List the friends or relatives who you would like have as your physical activity partners:

List other people from whom you would like support, and what support you would like them to give:

Now, ask them!

Summary

Get friends and family to support your efforts.
Get friends and family to join you.

Preparation: I'm getting ready to start!

Planning for an active life

Things just don't get done by chance. We have to plan and organize most things in life if we want to get them done. So why should fitting physical activity and physical activity into a busy daily schedule be any different?

The preparation stage is when the individual has started planning some activity, perhaps participating now and again, but have not reached the level they have set themselves.

By planning at the beginning, you are much more likely to get started and be able to keep going. Planning should involve an analysis of those things that are likely to influence your physical activity, and these are in 3 main areas:

- your physical surroundings
- your friends and social circle
- your own thoughts

Thinking and Planning Task

Think about your PHYSICAL SURROUNDINGS as far as physical activity is concerned. Write down those things that are positive, those that are negative, and possible actions which you might be able to take as a result of this.

POSITIVE   ACTIONS
eg physical activity facility close by   use facility

NEGATIVE   ACTIONS
eg boring walkiing routes   walk with a colleague
to work   or an iPod

Another Thinking and Planning Task

Think about your SOCIAL SURROUNDINGS (the people around you) as far as physical activity is concerned. Write down the things that are positive, those that are negative, and possible actions which you might be able to take as a result of this.

POSITIVE

eg partner also physically active

ACTIONS

be physical activity together

NEGATIVE

eg if I'm not at work I have to look after the baby

ACTIONS

walk with the baby in a sling

Thinking Task

Think about your OWN THOUGHTS as far as physical activity is concerned. Write down those thoughts that are positive, those that are negative, and possible actions which you might be able to take as a result of this.

POSITIVE   ACTIONS

eg I feel better after physical activity   plan activity
                                                   early in the day

NEGATIVE   ACTIONS

eg I haven't time to be active   remind yourself
                                                   that physical activity
                                                   makes you more
                                                   productive

Obviously, having physical surroundings that are not helpful for physical activity (e.g. busy city streets), makes activity that little bit more difficult. However, there WILL be positive things to highlight about your area, so use this to your advantage. Also get your friends to support your efforts. If you are surrounded by positive encouragement, and people who are also physically active, this will help a great deal.

Finally, why should positive personal thoughts help?

Well, we have known for many years that positive thinking can boost behaviour, and negative thoughts can make us apathetic and unmotivated. You need to change negative thoughts into positive ones. In hypnotherapy, this is called "reframing". Here are some examples:

NEGATIVE STATEMENTS	POSITIVE STATEMENTS
I'm naturally fat and all this physical activity won't make a difference	I may never be slim, but I can control my body weight
I'm just not the sporty type	I don't have to be good at sport to get the health benefits from physical activity
I ate a bar of chocolate today so really I've blown my weight control activity programme!	The occasional treat won't matter .... I'll do some physical today anyway
I'm going to get fit for the beach this summer	I have an on-going physical activity programme that will help keep me in shape for the summer and beyond

Take Action
Write down some positive words or thoughts for yourself and pin them up in a place where you will see them regularly (eg on the fridge door).

Summary

1. look at your physical surroundings
2. look at your social surroundings
3. look at what you say to yourself
4. make these 3 things positive and work in your favour.

Breaking down the barriers

There are barriers that stand in the way for all of us in many aspects of our lives. Physical activity is no different. Research has shown that the most common barriers that people think exist for physical activity are

- lack of time
- inconvenience/obstacles
- the physical effort required
- health or illness problems

Answer the questions in the next exercise and rate your physical activity barriers.

Barriers

In each case, circle the number that best describes you.

A major reason why I might not be physically active is:

	NO!	no	?	yes	YES!
1. I lack motivation	1	2	3	4	5
2. I'm too lazy	1	2	3	4	5
3. I'm too busy	1	2	3	4	5
4. I don't have enough time	1	2	3	4	5
5. For health reasons or due to physical disability	1	2	3	4	5
6. Because of illness	1	2	3	4	5
7. It's too inconvenient	1	2	3	4	5
8. Lack of facilities	1	2	3	4	5

Scoring:
Add up your scores as follows and write them below:
Q1 + Q2 = EFFORT SCORE   _
Q3 + Q4 = TIME SCORE   _
Q5 + Q6 = HEALTH SCORE   _
Q7 + Q8 = OBSTACLES SCORE   _

Using your barriers scores.

Scores of 6 or more highlight possible barriers to your being more active. Each one will be dealt with now, but you need only concentrate on the ones where you scored 6 points or more.

Effort

Remember that exercise is often about getting or keeping fit. Therefore, most people, when they hear the word 'exercise', think 'ugh, sweat, pain, effort!'. But, it need not be like that. Physical activity need not be like army training or a punishment for being last out on the field for PE! In fact, it's better to think about physical activity rather than just exercise.

On this point, let us digress! Can you believe that some physical education teachers still use exercise as punishment?! It is because of this that many people think of exercise as nasty and unpleasant. The PE students and teachers that Stuart has worked with over the years are told that such a strategy is absolute nonsense, but it still happens!

It's like parents punishing their children by giving them an apple! (If they did, how often do you think the child would choose an apple when given a choice?)

We must make physical activity pleasant and enjoyable and never use it as punishment!

Back to the point .....! Some years ago, the BBC asked Stuart to advise them on the programme "It doesn't have to hurt!". This was a series of seven programmes of 10 minutes each, presented by June Whitfield. What a great title! It tells us that physical activity need not be blood, sweat and tears. Absolutely right!

Such a message is an important one for those thinking that physical effort is a real barrier to participation.

Remember - physical activity, as we defined it at the beginning of this book, is any movement above resting levels, so effort shouldn't be too much of a problem there! Exercise, however, is usually more vigorous and will require some physical effort. But even exercise can range from fairly easy to very vigorous - it's your choice. If you think it will be too hard, choose activities that can be done easily to start with, like walking.

Time

This is the most common of the barriers, but, usually, it is not the actual amount of time that available in the day that matters, but how much time you think you have. One research study showed that those who took part in physical activity had just as much 'free time' as those who did not take part.

If you scored high on the time barrier, go back and look again at the lifestyle planning exercises.
You can also fit physical activity into your daily routine quite easily, and with little extra time needed, by cutting down on labour-saving devices and transport.

TYPICAL ACTIVITY	ACTIVE ALTERNATIVE
Bus to work	Walk last two stops
Car to work	Walk in, bus back
Use lift	Use the stairs
Stand on escalators	Walk the escalators or take the stairs
Sit through a lunch break	Take a 10 min walk, then have lunch

Health

Of course, if you are ill you really shouldn't take vigorous exercise, and your doctor should advise you on the best thing to do. Sometimes, though, it can be vicious circle: "I'm not healthy, so I can't be physically active; I'm not physically active, and my health is getting worse".

There will be many genuine reasons for not being as physically active as you could be, including injury, illness or disability. However, do check with an expert and see if there is something that might be beneficial for you. Physical activity is often a form of rehabilitation from injury! For older adults, different forms of physical activity might be best, such as chair-based exercises, arm strengthening exercises to assist raising from a chair, or joint mobility exercises to help maintain independent living.

Obstacles

Many people think that physical activity is inconvenient or that facilities are not available. Of course, for some people it may not be easy fitting it in, but the planning physical activities in this book should help. In fact you should actively try to make physical activity as convenient as possible!

Fitting it into your everyday schedule (see the table above) is one way. Also, you don't have to have flashy physical activity facilities! Walking can be done almost anywhere. Sometimes facilities can be a problem, so schedule their use when it is least inconvenient, at weekends for example.

Better still, most "lifestyle activities" (those done as part of normal living) have few obstacles, such as walking more than at present.

Summary

1. identify your barriers to physical activity
2. plan for action in minimizing these barriers.

Think about it !

Setting targets and goals: the road to physical activity is paved with good intentions!

When preparing to be physically active it is important to set goals and targets and to monitor behaviour and progress. Settings goals has been highly successful in many different areas, including work, schools and in sport. It can really help you achieve your desire to be physically active.

Why do goals work?

Goals help us concentrate and focus on the important things that determine our behaviour. For example, if you set yourself the goal of walking to work every Monday and Friday, you are much more likely to think about exactly how you will organize this than if you said 'I will try to walk to work sometime'.

This tells us that goals should be specific so that we can check if we have achieved them or not

Guidelines on the setting of goals

1.   Set reasonably challenging but realistic targets for yourself.

2.   Focus on participation in physical activity, rather than your actual performance. This means that you should concentrate on things like the number of times each week that you are active or the length of time you are physically active rather than how many press-ups you can do or how fast you walk a set

route. Target and reinforce your involvement first - if you want different outcomes, like fitness, these will follow.

3.   Stay flexible with your goals and modify them with experience.

4.   Think of goal-setting as a stairway, as shown here. You should have a long-term goal (top of stairs), but this will take some time to reach . You also need more reachable goals along the way.

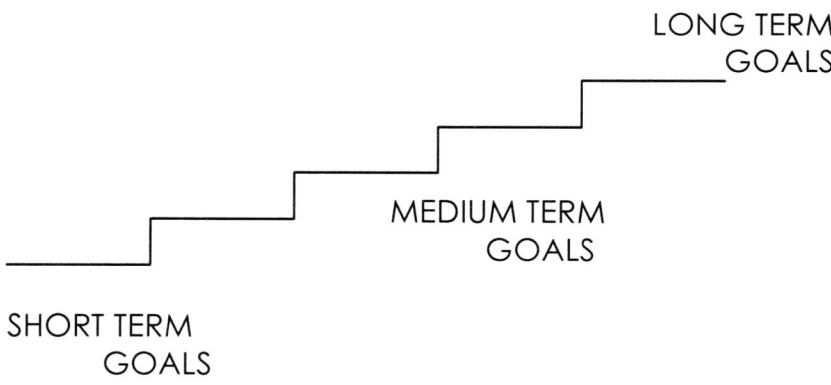

LONG TERM
GOALS

MEDIUM TERM
GOALS

SHORT TERM
GOALS

Set yourself targets related to your involvement, rather than physical performance. Give each a priority rating (1=high). State how you are going to try to achieve it - this is the action column.

Here is an example for you to use as a basis for your own goal-setting:

Target	Priority	Action
to walk to work three times a week until Christmas	1	Write into diary; refuse lifts on Mondays, Wednesdays and Fridays!
to swim with Jane on Tuesday after work	2	Phone Jane to arrange; keep Tuesday early evenings free in diary

Goal-setting Task

Long-Term Goals

Write in your goals for your physical activity and health for the future. Take a long term view if you wish, or just the next year. Your action should state what you intend to do towards this target over the **next two months**.

Target	Priority	Action

Medium-Term Goals

Do the same again; this time your targets are for the next three months. Your action should state what you intend to do towards this target **this week**.

Target   Priority   Action

Short-Term Goals

Do the same again; this time your targets are for next week. Your action should state what you intend to do **today** to help meet these targets!

Target	Priority	Action

You should check the guidelines again to help you set goals in the right way if you are in doubt. Also, you will need to use the short-term goals sheet quite often so you may want to make extra copies or copy it out for use later.

Keep these tables in view and keep reminding yourself of the targets.

Summary

1.   set realistic, reasonably challenging and measurable (specific) goals

2.   set goals for the long, medium, and short term

3.   set goals for participation (ie DOING IT!) rather than for performance.

Action:
I'm doing it!

To be active you need
- confidence
- a feeling that you are in control
- enjoyment of activity
- good planning

Confidence

Common sense and psychological research agree on at least one thing! Confidence is important! This is true for all areas of life. Commentators will often say that someone in sport has a loss of confidence, and that this has affected their game, even though they are probably physically exactly the same as before. Even something like asking someone for a date requires confidence - 'go on, pluck up the courage' we might be told. In other words, 'have confidence'.

Psychologists have studied confidence from many different angles, and they too agree that it is very important. Changing levels of confidence has been used to help overcome phobias, reduce anxiety, increase work performance, improve sports performance, and even recover from major surgery.

OK, so you're convinced! So what can you do about it?

It is best to see confidence in at least four ways, each of which can be altered to help boost confidence:

Being Successful

Success leads to success, but how do I get success in the first place? Certainly, the most important confidence builder is to have success. This may require you to start gradually and build slowly. There is a famous example of this step-by step approach in sport when an American swimmer said that he needed to cut 4 seconds from his time to win the Olympics. But 4 seconds is a big margin in international swimming (low confidence?). So, he broke it down and said that 4 seconds over 4 years was only 1 second each year (higher confidence), half a second for six months (higher confidence), 0.003 of a second each day ("I can do that!"). 0.003 is the time it takes to blink an eye!

Another way to experience success is to think of success as personal improvement rather than being better than someone else. We can all improve - we cannot always win! And, very importantly: PLEASE do notice your successes! Many of us have the tendency to discount our successes and concentrate on our "failures".

As far as physical activity is concerned, think of success as being involved on a regular basis - not being fitter or a better performer than your friend at work. This way you are likely to think about strategies that will help yourself - more effort, better planning, change of activity etc.

Seeing Success in Others

Often we think "I can't do that!". We watch others and think that what they do is beyond us. Yet often we watch superior people, like the 'perfect' models on physical activity videos, or sports stars in keepfit books.

You will best build confidence by watching people similar to you. Although Chris Hoy and Jessica Ennis may be motivating and entertaining to watch, they are not like you or us (well, not like us anyway!), so it's an unfair comparison. Work at your own level and fit into a group that you feel comfortable with.

Being Positive

Being positive will also help confidence and so keep saying positive things to yourself about your exercise and active lifestyle. If you have physical activity partners,
say positive things to them too! If others say negative things to you, think about it, see if there is anything to learn, if so, learn it, and if not, just let it go.

Again we are looking for positivity about participation rather than just high performance.

Stuart remembers making this point to a group of teachers in a lecture on the psychology of exercise, fitness and health in Birmingham. Stuart and the group then went downstairs into a sports hall where the teachers had the chance to try out a number of different activities that they might use with their pupils. One was the 20 metre progressive shuttle run fitness test. You have to run between two lines 20m apart but arrive at the line at the same time as a 'bleep' noise from a tape recorder. The bleeps come quite slowly at first, but gradually speed up until, after about 10-15 minutes, most people are unable to reach the line in time. This gives an estimate of your stamina performance.

During the lecture Stuart mentioned that it was important to reinforce the effort that people made in physical activity, and not just their performance. But what happened in the shuttle run? People dropped out of the run as it got quicker, and eventually only one teacher was left running. As soon as he finished he received a tremendous round of applause! Quite right too you're probably saying, but what about the others? It could be that the first person to drop out put in 95% effort, but had only 50% 'ability', whereas the last runner to drop out and the one to receive all of the credit, might have run at 75% effort but with 90% 'ability'! Who would you applaud? Both I hope, although it could be argued that the 95% effort is more creditable.

So, please, help peoples' confidence by saying good things to them about their own efforts - hopefully they will return the compliment.

Staying Relaxed

Being relaxed and free of anxiety and worries is the other side of the coin from confidence. Psychologists have found confidence can be built up in stressful situations if people learn to relax first.

In physical activity, you may need to relax in order to feel confident. For example, some people are reluctant to go to physical activity classes or clubs. Many report that they feel uneasy at the prospect, probably because they think they are not 'good enough'. But, you don't have to be 'good' to be physically active! Relaxation might help here.

Your hypnotherapist will be able to help you with any confidence and relaxation issues.

Confidence Rating

This exercise will ask you to think of at least two situations - one is to do with structured exercise, and one to do with everyday physical activity.
Write in below a type of exercise you would like to do over the next few months on a regular basis. It could be jogging, cycling, swimming, a sport, dancing, etc, etc.

Exercise = _____

Now write in 5 levels for this exercise, such as jog 5 mins, jog 10 mins etc., and rate your confidence for each level using a scale from 1 to 5, where:
1 = not at all confident   2 = not confident
3 = neutral   4 = confident
5 = totally confident

Confidence Rating

Level 1   _____   Level 4   _____

Level 2   _____   Level 5   _____

Level 3   _____

Now do the same thing, but this time for a physical activity that is part of your normal day, such walking, climbing stairs etc.

Activity = _____

Again list 5 levels, such as climb one flight of stairs, walk last two bus stops etc., and rate your confidence for doing each level on a regular basis.

<u>Confidence Rating</u>

Level 1 _____   Level 4 _____

Level 2 _____   Level 5 _____

Level 3 _____

Having completed the confidence ratings you are now in a good position to use this information to your advantage.

Take the highest confidence rating you gave your exercise level and your physical activity level.

Now choose that as your level for the next few days or weeks. If this is too easy, then move up a level. However, remember, confidence is built on success - make sure you don't try to progress too fast.

Physical Rating

Another way of looking at confidence is to see how you rate yourself on different aspects of your life. You probably feel good about yourself in some areas, and not so good in others. This is also true, of course, for physical things. We might feel generally good about ourselves 'physically', with really high ratings related to our body shape, but lower ratings about our sports ability.

In other words, we have levels of confidence and feelings about different aspects of our selves that might be related to physical activity.

The physical ratings scale gives you the chance to assess how you feel about yourself in three main areas:

- sports competence
- your physical condition
- your body

Rating Your Physical Self

Please circle the number for each statement which describes how you feel about yourself.

	NO!	no	?	yes	YES!
1. I feel I am good at most sports	1	2	3	4	5
2. I feel confident when taking part in most sports	1	2	3	4	5
3. I feel confident & at ease in most places of exercise	1	2	3	4	5
4. Compared to most, I feel that my physical condition and fitness is quite high	1	2	3	4	5
5. I feel that my body is in good shape and is quite attractive	1	2	3	4	5
6. I feel confident about the appearance of my body	1	2	3	4	5

Scoring:

Q1 + Q2 = Sports score = _____

Q3 + Q4 = Physical condition score = _____

Q5 + Q6 = Body score = _____

<u>Sports competence</u>: if you scored 6 or above on the sports scale, you should think about taking part in sports or physical activities where competence is measured in some way. You are quite confident about this area and you may find sports motivating.

<u>Physical condition</u>: if you scored 6 or above on this scale, you think that you are quite fit and you feel confident about going to exercise classes, fitness clubs etc. These types of exercises, therefore, may appeal to you and you may find them motivating.

<u>Body</u>: if you scored 6 or more on the body scale you feel quite good about your own body. If you scored below 6, however, you may want to be physically active to change things. Activities good for losing body fat are any that involve continuous and prolonged movement, like walking, jogging, swimming etc.

If you wish to tone up your body, you may wish to try muscle toning physical activity programmes available in health clubs, or just muscle toning at home with simple exercises that involve your own bodyweight as resistance.

Summary: Confidence

1. get success by starting slowly; define success as personal improvement

2. watch others like you being successful

3. say positive things to yourself and others

4. relax

5. choose activities that you are comfortable with and confident about.

Feeling in control

Related to the feeling of confidence is the feeling of being in control. Saying "I can do this!" is saying "I'm in control". We can look at control from several different angles.

The most obvious one is the control we think we can operate ourselves - things are in our control. However we may also think that control is held by others ('the doctor will cure me'), or that control doesn't really exist and that luck will determine what happens.

From a motivational point of view it is often better to feel in control yourself rather than expect someone else or luck to decide.

So when do we feel most in control?

Usually when we feel confident that we can do something, and usually do it well. This means that you will be in control of maintaining your regular walking programme when you have a well-planned schedule of when you are going to walk, how far, who with, etc etc. You will feel less in control when you rely on others to do things for you.

"I will wait until John phones to see if I'll run today".

Turn this around to:

"I will run today at noon, unless John phones to arrange another time".

Ratings of Control

	NO!	no	?	yes	YES!
1. I have the power to change my physical activity routine	1	2	3	4	5
2. Whether or not I exercise is entirely up to me	1	2	3	4	5
3. The physical activity I do is influenced by other people around me	1	2	3	4	5
4. Friends, relatives or other people determine my physical activity because of their influence on me	1	2	3	4	5
5. Whether or not I am active is a matter of luck	1	2	3	4	5
6. The amount of physical activity I get is related to chance or fate	1	2	3	4	5

Scoring:
Q1 + Q2 = Personal score   = _____
Q3 + Q4 = Other people score   = _____
Q5 + Q6 = Luck score   = _____

If you scored 6 or more on the PERSONAL scale this shows that you think that physical activity is under your own control. This is good and shows you some confidence to keep planning your activity in the future.

If you scored 6 or above on the OTHER PEOPLE scale you have a tendency to think that others, like friends or family, are quite an influence on whether you are active or not. Of course, this could be positive as long as these friends and family influence you in the right way! If you feel that this is not a good thing, remember that your own actions will be more easily controlled by you rather than by others, so try not to be too reliant on them getting you to be active and persuade them to support you.

Finally, if you scored 6 or more on the LUCK scale. you think that luck has quite an influence. I'm sure you are right up to a point. Chance events will occur, but remember you have no control over these, so it is better to focus on your ability to plan and control. This will help motivation and staying active! As a golfer once said, 'the more I try, the luckier I get'!

Summary: Control

1. feeling in control helps build confidence.

2. control can be influenced by you.

3. you might think other people have control over some your actions, in which case try to get their support.

4. you might think that little control is possible because of luck, but this is unlikely to be helpful.

Enjoying physical activity

Basil Fawlty once mocked his wife Sybil by suggesting that her subject on Mastermind should be "stating the bleedin' obvious!". Perhaps saying that enjoyment is important to staying active is stating the bleedin' obvious !

Nevertheless, we are going to say it!

Too often we think negatively about physical activity. Remember our earlier comments about physical activity being used as punishment?
An example to illustrate this could come from the Army. Many young recruits are put through exercise as a form 'character building' and 'self-discipline', as well as physical fitness. Even though these recruits may achieve much-improved levels of fitness, they are quite likely to say, on leaving the Army, 'I'm glad I don't have to exercise like that any more!'

You could say that the Army wins the battle of fitness (they get young people fit), but lose the war of exercise and health (because on leaving, most have been put off physical activity for life). If we are doing the Army a disservice, we apologize - but you get the point, we hope.

Many human behaviours reflect the 'enjoyment principle' - within reason, if we enjoy it, we do it! Smoking is a good example. Many smokers know that they are damaging their health, but they find it very difficult to stop because they enjoy it. The same could be said for drinking and eating habits.

One big difference between smoking, drinking and eating, and physical activity, is that only physical activity involves some physical effort. You may remember that effort is seen to be a barrier to physical activity by many people. This makes it particularly important to make physical activity a rewarding experience if people are to carry on.

What is enjoyment?

Try coming up with a definition. It's not easy is it? It is an everyday word that we understand but find difficult to put into words.

However, help is at hand. A psychologist by the unusual name of Dr Csikszentmihalyi (let's call him Dr C, to avoid typing that again) has studied enjoyment in various activities, including composers of music, dancers, rock climbers, chess players, and basketball players. He found that maximum enjoyment was achieved when the challenge of the task was matched by the capabilities of the individual. In other words, the "I can!" feeling is true here also, as with feelings of control and confidence.
Indeed, Dr C said that the types of activities where enjoyment was experienced, and where people would participate for hours sometimes, were those where some control was felt.

So what happens when the challenge is not met by the skills of the individual?

Dr C suggested that when the challenge is too low and easy, boredom sets in. When the challenge is too high or difficult, anxiety sets in. Not surprisingly, he called his book on the topic 'Beyond Boredom and Anxiety'. So, match the activity with your own levels of skills and competence; that way enjoyment should be boosted.

Enjoyment Rating

Write down some types of physical activity or sports that you think you will enjoy. Put them in order of enjoyment (1=most enjoyable).

1. _____

2. _____

3. _____

4. _____

5. _____

Summary: Enjoyment

1. find activities where your abilities meet the challenge

2. choose activities that make you feel good mentally.

Maintenance:
I'm there and will stay there!

Staying active - this is often the hardest part!

Quite a few people get started and have positive intentions in the early stages. However, we think that of those who start a physical activity programme in a keep-fit class or fitness club, only about 50% will still be going several months later.

Remember that we said earlier that only about 30% of the British adult population take part in physical activity that is likely to improve their health?

This figure (which is quite low - and the government have said that it should increase if we are to become a healthier nation), is the result of people not being able to <u>stay active</u>. It's the 'New Year resolution' statement again. After a few weeks, everything's back to where it was before.

So this means that staying active is a critical period in your plan.

Some who quit may start up again later, but even so there is the danger that once you get started, something comes along to stop you. We need to prepare to avoid quitting!

It is almost impossible, for even the most dedicated participants, not to have some periods of inactivity due to illness, injury or something else. So, don't feel guilty about occasional lapses, many of which will be for very good reasons. To help prevent yourself quitting though, here are some guidelines.

Intensity of physical activity

Have you ever been to an exercise class where the exercise leader seemed more interested in making you suffer than enjoy the physical activity?

Fiona finished a class once and was told that next week would be tougher because it had to hurt to get improvement!

Rubbish!

We doubt if any of that group improved because we would expect most not to come back. Fiona didn't! The intensity of the physical activity routine can be related to dropout. Intense and vigorous sessions will only appeal to a small minority, like those training for sport. Research also shows that the 'feel good' effect of physical activity is much less, or even negative ('feel bad') when the intensity is too high.

You need to avoid doing too much too soon. Take the physical activity at your own pace, and make gradual and comfortable changes. You should not feel sore or too tired the next day. This is why people are much more likely to stick with more moderate forms of physical activity.

How to regulate the intensity of physical activity

Intensity refers to how hard the physical activity is. This could be reflected physically, like a pounding heart or tired muscles. Of course, we can feel these physical changes occurring so we are able to rate our overall effort or physical exertion, subjectively. The Effort Rating Scale shows one way of doing this:

6	No effort at all
7	
8	
9	Very light
10	
11	Light
12	
13	Fairly hard
14	
15	Hard
16	
17	Very hard
18	
19	Extremely hard
20	Maximum effort

This scale was developed by a Swedish researcher, Dr Gunnar Borg, and it can be used to help you regulate and control how hard you exercise. Of course, most of the time you will exercise simply at a level that feels comfortable, but if you want to try to improve your stamina, you should try to keep exercising for about 15-20 minutes at a level you rate between 12 and 15 on the scale. This will be roughly the same as having a heart beat of about 120-150 beats per minute for the 'average man'.

Equally, you may wish to simply be more active and not take too much notice of the effort involved. For example, you might choose to walk to work more often without rating your effort. That said, it's still better to walk briskly which is about 12 on the scale.

Taking it in stages

Most people think that they should go straight into physical activity with the goal of improving fitness.

Wrong!

The first few weeks should be about getting used to physical activity again. This is sometimes called the 'starter phase'. Learn to adapt slowly and comfortably. Later on you can try to think about improvements in fitness where more effort is required, if that is what you want. This would be the 'growth phase'.

After that you might just be interested in maintaining this level. The table summarizes this for you:

Stages of a Physical activity Programme

Stage 1: Starter

   a) gradual and comfortable changes in
      physical activity and lifestyle
   b) start with light, enjoyable activities that
      create no discomfort
   c) don't think about trying to improve fitness

Stage 2: Growth

   a) learn about fitness improvement
   b) be flexible about fitness improvement
      guidelines
   c) keep emphasizing participation, not just
      performance

Stage 3: Maintenance

   a) further gains are probably not necessary for
      health
   b) health-related physical activity and sports
      training are different!

If you are interested in improving your fitness, there
are some guidelines for you to follow. Don't be too
rigid about these - they are merely a guide. If you
find them too easy or too difficult, modify them.

Remember that health-related fitness is made up several different parts. Let's look at developing fitness in three main areas:

- stamina
- muscle strength and endurance
- muscle flexibility

Improving Stamina With The F.I.T.T. Principle

FITT Component	Guidelines
F. Frequency: how often?	3-5 times per week
I. Intensity: how hard?	Heart rate between 60-85% of maximum (see below).
T. Time: how long?	20 minutes or more, continuously.
T. Type (of exercise)	Exercise using legs or whole body, such as running, swimming, cycling, walking.

Note: maximum heart rate = 220 - age. 60% of maximum is (220 - age) x 0.6

Improving Muscle Strength And Endurance With The F.I.T.T. Principle

FITT Component	Guidelines
F. Frequency: how often?	2-3 times per week.
I. Intensity: how hard?	Comfortable muscle effort, but a little more than usual. Moderate fatigue to be felt after 6-8 repetitions.
T. Time: how long?	20-30 minutes per session. Each exercise to be performed twice for 6-8 continuous repetitions.
T. Type (of exercise)	Anything where resistance is placed on the muscle. Could be weight training machines or apparatus, or just your own bodyweight.

Improving Muscle Flexibility With The F.I.T.T. Principle

FITT Component	Guidelines
F. Frequency: how often?	Can be done every day once some experience has been gained. Initially, every other day.
I. Intensity: how hard?	To the point of 'mild tension' in the stretched muscle.
T. Time: how long?	Each exercise: 10-30 seconds. Each session: 5-15 minutes.
T. Type (of exercise)	Stretch each major muscle in turn. Stretch slowly and then hold the stretch. Do not bounce in the stretch

Of course, it is not necessary that you exercise for fitness! It could be just as important to you just to take part without concerning yourself about fitness. That's fine. These guidelines are provided for those who might be interested.

Motivation

Let's go back to Sybil Fawlty - stating the bleedin' obvious: motivation is important for avoiding quitting!

Actually, motivation has been found to be very important in terms of whether people stay with an exercise programme, but is probably less important for more moderate forms of physical activity. First, try estimating your own motivation using the next task.

Remember that having high self-motivation is going to be more necessary for more vigorous types of exercise. But, even if you have a low score, you can simply plan your exercise and activity more so that you reduce the chance of quitting.

Motivation Rating Task

Circle one number for each statement as it best describes you. Be honest!

	NO!	no	?	yes	YES!
1. I can keep going at things even if they involve quite a lot of effort.	1	2	3	4	5
2. I don't work any harder than I have to.	1	2	3	4	5
3. I'm just not the type of person to set goals.	1	2	3	4	5
4. I'm good at making decisions and keeping to them.	1	2	3	4	5
5. I easily get put off.	1	2	3	4	5
6. I can persist through discomfort.	1	2	3	4	5
7. I have a lot of willpower.	1	2	3	4	5
8. I'm basically lazy.	1	2	3	4	5

Scoring:

Score questions 1,4,6, and 7 as they are, BUT score questions 2,3,5, and 8 in reverse so that a score of 1 becomes 5, 2 becomes 4 etc.

Now add all eight responses (remember to reverse the scoring on four of them!)

Your Motivation Score = _____

30-40 Good! You seem the type who could easily stick an exercise programme!

20-29 This is OK, but you might need help at times. The exercises and advice in this book are designed for this!

0-19 You are prone to quit physical activity, so make plans nor:' Follow the advice here - it's written for you!

One form of motivation that is often used is the giving of prizes and gifts as a reward. This is called 'external motivation' as it comes from outside of yourself. Where the motivation comes from 'within', such as being motivated to do well at something simply because you want. to and enjoy it, this is called 'internal motivation'.

Internal motivation is usually stronger and lasts for longer than external motivation. But sometimes external motivation can be very useful indeed. For example, if you scored low on the motivation scale, external motivation in the form of rewards will be needed to keep you going.

But don't rely on these types of motivation for ever. Let us illustrate why.

Once upon a time there was a girl, Susie, who enjoyed playing outside her house everyday by skipping, running and cycling. Her parents then saw a TV programme on the importance of being physically active. As a result, they thought that it would be a good idea to encourage Susie so they offered her £1 for each week where she spent at least 3 days playing in this way. Susie was delighted! Money for old rope! After a few months, however, Susie was told by her parents that they were a little hard up for cash and that their reward would be only 50p a week. Susie accepted this. However, when a few more weeks went by and Susie's parents explained that their cash flow was even worse and that the reward would be only 5p, Susie retorted "only 5p - I'm not going to play for only 5p. I'll go in and watch TV!" She lived a sedentary and unhappy life every after!

What happened is that Susie, although quite happy to be physically active without a reward to start with, then started to play for the reward. When it was reduced, the incentive to play (the money) was no longer there.

Be warned - use external rewards with care and only to help get over difficult periods or to reward people for doing a specific job really well. Try to encourage more internal motivation if you can.

Reinforcement and punishment

External rewards are one type of reinforcement. Enjoyment is another. Reinforcement is anything that makes it more likely that the action will occur again in the future.

Here are some examples:
- praise
- rewards
- success

The other side of the same coin is punishment. This is something that reduces the chance of the action occurring again. Examples are:
- unpleasant feelings
- physical pain
- negative criticism

Public recognition and reinforcement often goes on in fitness clubs. For example, a notice might be posted that says:

****

Congratulations!
-this week's 20 mile joggers are:

Jane Marple
Harry Potter
Robert Langdon

****

Punishment must not be associated with physical activity. We have already made this point, but it is important that we change peoples' views on physical activity, and one way is to let them know that it should not be punishing!

Given the cautionary note earlier about the use of external rewards, you must be careful using such strategies. However, they do have their place. We are all motivated by recognition for having done a job well!

Even if it is only recognized by you!

For such situations, rewards may be helpful. However, try to make the reward reasonably healthy! Getting drunk to reward yourself for having completed your first 1 mile run might be a little inappropriate.

Catching the eye

Another motivational technique that has been found to work is when you place an eye-catching sign or note that reminds you to do something.

A group of researchers watched how many people used the stairs instead of the escalator or lift. Then put up a cartoon of a heart running up the stairs with the message "your heart needs physical activity - here's your chance". The researchers then watched again and found that the use of the stairs was much greater.

Weighing up the pros and cons

A useful strategy to avoid dropping out of physical activity is to consider the pros and cons of sticking with it or dropping out. Try this now by using the decision chart.

Fill in the chart for both the short term and the long term.

Now use this information to help you avoid quitting. Highlight the advantages and positive features of both short and long term involvement. Plan your strategies with these in mind. Keep reminding yourself of these positive things.

Task

Decision Chart: Write in the pros (positive) and cons (negative) of sticking with or quitting exercise and physical activity.

Short Term

	Sticking	Quitting
Pro		
Con		

Long Term

	Sticking	Quitting
Pro		
Con		

Changes in circumstances

Our circumstances change with age. We leave school, get a new job, move house, get married, have children, change job, children leave home, retire etc etc. Nothing stays the same. Any one of these stages in your life could affect the amount of physical activity you manage to get.

You need to be aware of potential problem periods so that you are better able to cope when they arrive. There are no easy answers here as each person will be different. However, planning will always be required to stay active and particularly when other people are involved or time is very short.

Be cooperative with others and get their support. There will also be other times, such as during retirement, when time may be more available or flexible.

Summary

1. really vigorous exercise can put people off and cause dropout. Learn to regulate a comfortable level for you.
2. those high in motivation should be able to stick with physical activity quite easily. Those who are less motivated may need extra help or take part only in more moderate forms of activity initially.

3. use rewards to say 'well done!' rather than as a bribe.
4. don't make physical activity a punishing experience.
5. use eye-catching signs and symbols to remind you about your activity.
6. think about the pros and cons of staying active or not staying active. Highlight the advantages.
7. things change with time. Plan accordingly.

Starting Up Again!

There are going to be times when you cannot be as physically active as you would like. There are also going to be times when you need to resume participation.

Many of the guidelines offered already in this book, of course, will apply here, but also you need to remain positive about your previous participation. In particular you will need to go back to the sections of the book on CONFIDENCE (p 69) and GOAL-SETTING (p 61) so that you are better able to cope with the new situation of being less active and then be able to plan for future activity.

Stuart's research has shown that the way people think about why they stopped or continued participation in an physical activity programme can be important for motivation. If you have to stop exercising for a while, avoid making negative statements about yourself. In other words, don't be self-critical. Look to positive things in the future that you can control and change and so that physical activity becomes more likely.

Thinking Task

Think about why you have become less active. Perhaps you have just had several weeks of little or no activity. Write down the main reason that you think this has come about:

Main reason:

Now think again about the reason you have just written down. Think about it while you answer each of these questions by circling one number on each line:

1. The reason listed:

Reflects an aspect   5   4   3   2   1   Reflects an aspect
of yourself   of your situation

2. The reason listed:

Is temporary   5   4   3   2   1   Is permanent

3. The reason listed:

Is under my control   5   4   3   2   1   Is not under my
                                              control

Your ratings reflect whether you are well placed, or not so well placed, to deal with your current inactivity.
Question 1 = INTERNAL SCORE Question 2 = UNSTABLE SCORE Question 3 = CONTROL SCORE

The best ratings you can have are when you circle high numbers for each scale. Why? Because this means that your inactivity is seen to be due to factors that are to do with yourself (question 1: internal), that are temporary (Q2: unstable) and that are under your control (Q3: control).

In other words, you are well placed to change these factors and bring about a more active lifestyle again. However, if you circled low numbers, you think that the reason is something unrelated to you, permanent, and not under your control; a very negative situation to be in.

This is when people are likely to give up forever. However, if this is the case, you must think again about possible reasons for your inactivity, and try to focus on aspects that you can change and control. There must be something! Then really work on this and look for ways of making progress.

The next exercise will help you pinpoint the problems that are stopping you being active at the moment and then finding alternatives.

Task

Write in the boxes below things that you find problems in relation to exercise or to being active. eg. not enough time; no place to exercise; nobody to exercise with; find it boring etc. etc.

In column 2, write in some possible alternatives that may help these problems; eg. if time is a problem think of the type of activity that can be done in a convenient place and time, such as home exercises, or walking to work.

In column 3, give a number out of 10 which rates your chances of actually doing what you say in column 2. If you are certain you will do it, give it 10 out of 10. If you are not so certain, perhaps the score will be 6 out of 10. Choose the activity with the highest score.

Column 1	Column 2	Column 3
Problems	Alternatives	Score

Summary

Obviously much of the advice already given in this book will also apply here. In addition:

1. think of why you have not been able to be so active. Think positively about these reasons and think of ways of controlling and changing such causes.
2. analyse the problems that seem to get in the way of you exercising. Choose the alternative that is most likely to be followed through.

Different Strokes For Different Folks!

The advice so far has been written in such a way that it should be applicable for most people, regardless of age, sex, abilities etc. However, there will also be special cases which require consideration, such as children or older adults. This section, therefore, will look at three issues as they apply to an active lifestyle:

- children
- older adults
- male/female differences.

Children & Youth

Much has been written about the apparent decline in physical activity in children, as well as their lack of fitness and increased fatness. We touched on this briefly in the introduction. The big question is, therefore, is there anything we can do to help children lead active and healthy lives?

Children are not active? Surely that's not true! Well, if you think about it a little more, the competing attractions of TV, videos and computers, coupled with increased perception of dangers of being out, playing near busy roads or being driven to school, mean that perhaps it's not so surprising that children choose more sedentary pursuits than their parents and grandparents, or that parents restrict children playing outside.

The reason that we have included a special section on children is to say that children are not mini adults and therefore may require a slightly different approach to that already outlined.

We need to help children 'switch on' to physical activity, exercise and sport while they are children in the hope that they will continue to be active when they are adults too.

Here are some suggestions for increasing children's chances of becoming active adults.

1. recognize that young children do start out in life as very active! They learn, somewhere, that activity is boring, hard work, unnecessary, not enjoyable etc etc. It is up to us, therefore, to keep them interested and stimulated in physical activity.

2. recognize that children want to exercise and play for a variety of reasons. These include:
- competition
- health
- fitness
- skill improvement
- friendship

In other words, not all children enjoy sport, nor enjoy physical activity for fitness and health. They will enjoy activities that are fun and are worthwhile.

3. When children are shown exercises for fitness and health, make them educational and fun! They will learn something worthwhile and will want to come back for more! This requires professional leadership from properly qualified teachers of physical education who are aware of the educational issues in the development of the child. There is no place for the drill sergeant here!

4. The emphasis must be on short-term benefits - children will understand and be motivated by this. Long-term benefits to health, while being important, will not motivate children to be active too often.

5. Avoid the 'gloom and doom' approach of telling kids to exercise because otherwise they will have a heart attack in 30 years time! Their reply will be: 'big deal - 30 years!'. Stress the benefits to them NOW! Many younger children will not be able to understand the longer-term benefits anyway. By all means teach children about the health benefits of physical activity, but don't expect that alone to motivate them!

6. Lead by example – be an active role model.

7. Be supportive of active children.

Older adults

The famous American comedian, George Burns, at the age of 90, went to see his doctor, who asked him what the trouble was. Burns replied "I've got a bad right knee". The doctor said that he should expect that sort of thing at his age. Burns retorted, "but my left knee's fine and it's the same age!".

Yes, we do stereotype older adults, and one such stereotype is that we become less active with age, less fit, and much fatter. Of course, this often does happen, often with good reason. For example, we do 'deteriorate' physically with age, and we can put on weight quite easily as we tend to burn less energy later in life.

But, the effects of ageing can be slowed down by having an active lifestyle. You will be able to do more things for a much longer time, have greater independence, and rely less on medical services.

One of the problems with the way we view exercise and physical activity for older adults is that we often encourage less activity! "Take it easy in retirement", "You've earned a rest" etc etc. However, the body is quite capable of a continued active life well after retirement age.

Here are some suggestions for staying active in the later years of life:

1. exercise and physical activity are not just for the young and very active!

2. encourage all people to be active, at least in some form - this should help reduce the stereotype that activity is not for older people.

3. adapt activities to suit your age and abilities. Older people will have to modify some things. That's ok - just don't stop altogether.

4. if in doubt, do check with your doctor. However, there are likely to be plenty of activities you can do, including dancing, sports, relaxation exercises, group exercise classes, expressive movement, yoga, walking etc etc.

5. YOU'RE NEVER TOO OLD TO BE PHYSICALLY ACTIVE!

A note on sex!

In our society, males and females are often portrayed in a stereotyped way. Also, many activities are stereotyped too. For example, is ballet a girls` or boys' activity? What about weight training?

Although some of you will answer 'neither', many will want to state a view that some activities are what we call 'sex-role appropriate'. In other words, we think that some activities are more 'appropriate' or 'suited' to one sex or the other.

The problem with believing that some activities are 'sex-role appropriate' you are helping to erect barriers to participation. If you think that weight training is 'not for girls', or exercise to music 'not for boys', this will not encourage girls or boys into being active.

Remember, that nearly all of the prejudice that exists in sport and physical activity is because of social values and stereotypes - not biological reasons. There is no biological reason why women shouldn't weight train!

Guidelines to help the promotion of exercise and physical activity for women and men:

1. believe that all activities are equally 'appropriate' for all types of people, regardless of sex.

2. avoid making stereotyped remarks about some activities. Encourage and praise activity - regardless of what it is.
3. people are motivated in many different ways. This may apply to women and men, but could equally apply to different men or different women. Don't assume men are like ....., and women are like

Other Healthy Pursuits

In this last section of the book, we will look briefly at some other aspects of a healthy lifestyle, all of which are likely to be part of your hypnotherapeutic sessions. These are:

- diet and nutrition
- alcohol
- non-smoking

We will not take too long on these as each one could fill a book, and your hypnotherapist will be able to advise you further. However, they will help give a more complete picture of a healthy lifestyle.

Diet & Nutrition

Many years ago, The Sunday Times produced one of their colour magazine series on health. This one was about many aspects of health and went by the title of the 'ABC Diet and Bodyplan'.

Quite catchy really. Yes, but it also contained a simple but classically effective message. ABC stood for -

A: Activity
B: Behaviour
C: Consumption

In other words, in order to maximize your chances of a healthy lifestyle, you should focus on appropriate physical activity and proper eating/drinking habits. In addition, you should try to modify and control your own behaviour - this is really what I have been saying throughout this book. So, ABC sums it up nicely.

What about C: Consumption? As with activity, you cannot ignore the 'behaviour' that goes with it. Controlling and modifying ones' eating is also to do with psychology. Before looking at that, a quick word about the types and functions of different food stuffs.

Healthy eating: Plus one, minus three

Many reports over the years have concluded that the average British diet should be modified in four ways:

- eat more fibre
- eat less fat
- eat less sugar
- eat less salt

Why eat more fibre?
>   Because it helps digestion and can reduce the risk of diabetes, gastrointestinal disease, and some types of cancers. Fibres are bulky foods and may help us eat less fatty and sugary foods.

124

Where do I find fibre?

In whole cereals (try to avoid the really sugary ones), leafy and root vegetables, fruit, pulses, and nuts.

Why eat less fat?

Because it can help reduce the risk of heart disease, particularly if you eat less saturated fat. Fat that is hard in room temperature, like the fat left after the Sunday joint has cooled, is saturated fat. So the fat in dairy products and animal meat is saturated, although white meat (poultry) and fish contain much less. Vegetable oils have less saturated fat too, although coconut and palm oil are exceptions.

Seeing that the average British diet has a high fat content, and much of this is saturated fat through meats and dairy products, reducing saturated fat intake is possible and should make a significant difference to our health.

Why eat less sugar?

It helps reduce the chances of being overweight which, in turn, will make you more susceptible to diabetes, high blood pressure and heart disease. It is also related to tooth decay. All this from sugar? Sugars are present in many foods, but they come in two main forms: simple and complex.
The simple sugars are those found in confectionery, many fizzy drinks, and sugar itself. These offer few nutritional benefits. In

contrast, 'energy', as well as other nutrients, can be gained from the complex sugars. These foods include: vegetables, fruit and grains (bread).

Why eat less salt?
Because it has been linked to high blood pressure, which, in turn, is linked to stroke and heart disease. In Britain we eat about 20 times as much salt as our bodies need, and about one third of our salt intake comes from the salt we add to our food. In other words, we have the potential to control salt intake quite easily.

Practical strategies for healthy eating

OK, OK! We believe you. The British diet is not so good after all! But what we can do about it?

Our suggestions will be based on simple strategies in much the same way as the sections on physical activity. The first and most important point is that good nutrition is more about thinking and behaviour than it is about supermarket prices or preferences.

In other words, we have learnt over the years that psychology can help us to adopt the 'right' behaviours so that we can:

- eat a well-balanced diet
- control our own body weight and fat.

Take 'dieting' as an example of the psychology of eating. How many 'diets' succeed? Very, very few - less than one percent if by 'success' you mean weight and fat loss that is sustained for a long period of time.

British people go on about two diets a year! If they were successful, they would only need one at most! So, 'diets' are more than just different eating and drinking routines.

By 'diet', I mean a change in your food and drink intake that is much less than you have been used to and is done with the goal of fat loss. The problem is that diets are often seen to be short-term. "I'm going on a diet" - presumably, therefore, there is a time when you come 'off' the diet. If so, what happens then? The weight gain and weight loss cycle starts all over again. 'The rhythm method of girth control', nutritionist Dr Meyer once called it!

It is actually quite unhealthy and it is better to stay moderately overfat than keep gaining and losing weight.

So what is the alternative?

The safer and more effective method if you wish to control bodyfat is to adopt comfortable and gradual changes in your physical activity and eating habits that are likely to be sustained for the rest of your life. To say "that's it - no more chocolate!" is probably quite unrealistic. But to say "OK, I will keep chocolate for certain times of the week only" is realistic. Very strict and unpleasant changes will never be sustained, so why start?

Earlier in this book we suggested that a good way to help you adopt physical activity was to analyse yourself in three ways:

- physical surroundings
- social surroundings
- personal thoughts

This can also be done for your eating and drinking behaviour. What things in your physical surroundings help or hinder your diet? (Here 'diet' means all of your food and drink).

What about your social surroundings? Are people always offering you food or suggesting you go for an alcoholic drink when you want to try to control your weight? What do you say to yourself about food and drink? Are you negative or positive in your thoughts? Try filling in the tables overleaf and analyzing these influences.

Diet Task

Think about your PHYSICAL SURROUNDINGS as far as your diet is concerned. Write down those things that are positive, and those that are negative, and possible actions which you might be able to take as a result of this.

POSITIVE   ACTIONS

eg always have a full fruit bowl   eat fruit if desperate between meals

NEGATIVE   ACTIONS

eg live next door to the pub   limit visits to 3 times per week and have low-cal tonic with gin

Diet Task

Think about your SOCIAL SURROUNDINGS (the people around you) as far as your diet is concerned. Write down the things that are positive, and those that are negative and possible actions which you might be able to take as a result of this.

POSITIVE   ACTIONS

eg partner hates chocolate   only eat chocolate
                                                   once a week

NEGATIVE   ACTIONS

Eg both of us love high fat   choose healthiest
    take aways   options and only
                                                   have one course

Diet Task

Think about your OWN THOUGHTS as far as your diet is concerned. Write down those thoughts that are positive, and those that are negative, and possible actions which you might be able to take as a result of this.

POSITIVE   ACTIONS

eg I feel better if I don't eat too much   use a small plate
                                            & don't have more

NEGATIVE   ACTIONS

eg I haven't time to plan healthy meals   plan your meals
                                            when doing
                                            something else
                                            (eg on the bus)
                                            & make meals simple

Physical surroundings: if you find that certain things trigger over-eating or over-drinking, try to change things. Many people eat watching TV. When they sit to watch TV later in the evening, even though they are full, they want to eat again. The TV has become a 'trigger' for food.

Social surroundings: if you find that some people are very positive and others less positive about your desire to eat and drink sensibly, try to control things when you are around these people.

Personal thoughts: for this we can again use reframing as described on p53. For example, "I cannot stop eating chocolate" can become "I can eat one chocolate bar per week; that way I can look forward to it, and really enjoy it"

Alcohol

One of the problem areas for many people trying to control their weight and lead a healthy life is over consumption of alcohol. We tend to drink more than we used to as alcoholic drinks are no longer kept just for special occasions. Also the increase in 'standard of living' has meant that alcohol can be bought by many more people. Over the past 25 years or so, our consumption of alcohol per person in Britain has doubled.

Drink Assessment Task

How much do you drink each week?

Drink	'Units'
1 pint normal strength beer/lager/cider	2
1 pint strong beer/larger	3
125 ml glass table wine	1
1 pub measure 'spirit'	1

Keep a diary for a week, or recall what you drank last week.

Now add up your units.

WOMEN:

* over 20 units is too much - you need to cut back
* 15-20 units is rather high - be careful and start to think of ways of controlling your drinking

MEN:

* over 35 units is too much - you need to cut back
* 20-35 units is rather high - be careful and start to think of ways of controlling your drinking.

There are many ways of cutting down, including analyzing when, where and under what circumstances you tend to over drink. These situations can then be modified or avoided. Other methods might include:

- keep a diary of your drinking and chart progress
- set yourself a target of controlled drinking
- keep below a daily figure
- drink slowly
- do other things when drinking
- reward yourself for success (not with a drink!)
- dilute spirits (eg with ice and/or mixers)
- drink spritzers rather than neat white wine

- eat before drinking
- drink water or a soft drink before alcohol
- choose low alcohol or alcohol-free drinks
- learn to say 'no thanks' to alcohol
- have several days in the week alcohol free
- start drinking later

If this is a problem area for you, ask your hypnotherapist to help you to take control. If it is a severe problem however, it may be that your therapist will refer you to a specialist.

Non-Smoking

"I'm dying for a cigarette". How true, yet many smokers, even though they know they are doing themselves great harm, continue to smoke.

Why?

This is a complex question, although presumably some form of enjoyment or reinforcement is present otherwise why bother? The tragedy is that tobacco-related diseases - and there are many - are wholly preventable. If we were a non-smoking country we would be considerably healthier.

Do you want the good news or the bad news?
First, here is the bad news:
- 106,000 people die in the UK each year as a result of cigarette smoking - about one every 12 minutes
- One in every two long term smokers will die prematurely from smoking related disease. Of those, half will die before the age of 70, cutting an average of 21 years from their expected life span
- Approximately 1200 people are admitted to hospital in the UK every day due to smoking
- Smokers are many, many times more likely to get cancer, including cancer of the lung, mouth, larynx, bladder and pancreas.

Here's the good news:
- smoking has declined and is now a minority pursuit
- over half the British adult population were smokers in the early 1970s, now about 21% are smokers

Why do people smoke?

Research has shown that if young people don't start smoking by their late teens, then they are not likely to become smokers. Very few people start as adults.

Some of the reasons are:

- To belong
- To look and feel grown up
- To rebel
- To look and feel "cool"
- As a stress reliever
- As a boredom reliever
- As something to do with the hands
- To lose weight/avoid gaining weight
- As an excuse to take a break

Why do people quit?

Most smokers claim they want to stop, and here are the most common reasons for wanting to do so:

- for health
- to save money

- because it is anti-social
- because the kids don't like it
- in order to get pregnant
- because of the smell
- because they are being controlled by smoking
- because there is no reason to continue

If any of these reasons apply to you, then you may like to ask your hypnotherapist to help you to quit. Hypnosis can be a very effective method for doing so. In fact research shows that it could be three times as effective as nicotine replacement, and five times as effective as using willpower alone.

However, many people carry on smoking due to fears of stopping. These include:

- Putting on weight
- Not being able to relax or have a break
- No longer being able to socialise with smoking friends
- Being irritable
- Change

All of these are surmountable! Tell your therapist what you fear, and they will work with you to find a solution.

Lightning Source UK Ltd.
Milton Keynes UK
22 May 2010

154559UK00001B/7/P